LITTLE-KNOWN FACTS ABOUT WELL-KNOWN STUFF

LITTLE-KNOWN FACTS ABOUT WELL-KNOWN STUFF

DAVID HOFFMAN

BARNES
& NOBLE

NEW YORK

Book Design by Sandi Silbert

ISBN-13: 978-0-7607-8529-4
ISBN-10: 0-7607-8529-5

Printed and bound in the United States of America.

10 9 8 7 6 5 4 3 2

Using the highest
strength grade of Velcro,
a 160-pound person will
stick to a wall with only
a four-inch square.

OFF! and similar
mosquito repellents don't really
repel—they hide you.
The spray blocks the
mosquito's sensors so they don't
realize you are there.

Polaroid photographs are completely developed when they come out of the camera. It is the process of the opaque coating that covers them slowly turning transparent (and allowing the image underneath to appear) that gives the impression that the picture is developing before your eyes.

The dyes of a Polaroid photo
are still wet immediately after
developing. If you quickly
slap the photo onto your arm
or back, it will result in a
photo-realistic temporary tattoo.

Pencils aren't hexagonal because it makes them easier to grip. They were originally cut that shape to keep them from rolling off desks and tables.

Manhole covers
are round because that is the
only common shape
that won't
fall through a hole if it gets
tilted sideways.

The toothpick

is the item on which people

most often choke.

15

A Boeing
747 airliner holds
57,285 gallons
of fuel.

When glass breaks,

the cracks move

faster than

3,000 miles per hour.

The Ramses brand
condom is named after
the great Pharaoh Ramses II,
who fathered over
160 children.

Duck tape was originally green and developed by Johnson & Johnson for the U.S. military, which wanted a waterproof tape that would keep the moisture out of (and blend in with) their ammunition cases. During the postwar housing boom, it was discovered that it was also good for heating and air conditioning duct work, so the color was changed from army green to silver, and duck tape became *duct* tape.

The homes that line Wisteria Lane—which were lived in by the Cleavers, the Hardy Boys, and the men of *Animal House* before they were rebuilt and remodeled for the *Desperate Housewives*—were first bought by Universal Studios from the city of Los Angeles, which was going to destroy them to make way for Dodger Stadium.

21

Evergreen Terrace,

the street the Simpsons live on,

is also the street

Matt Groening grew up on in

Portland, Oregon.

The voices for many of the characters on *The Simpsons*, according to the actors who do them, are nothing more than "bad celebrity impressions": Moe Syzlak is Al Pacino, Louie (the cop) is based on Sylvester Stallone, and Mayor Quimby was inspired by John F. Kennedy.

"Mandyville" is entertainment industry slang for the place that television characters go when they disappear from a series without explanation. It is derived from Moira Kelly's character Mandy Hampton, who vanished from *The West Wing* after the first season with no mention of whatever happened to her.

25

In the pilot episode of
Curb Your Enthusiasm,
Larry and Cheryl made reference to
the fact that they had several kids,
even though they were never
shown. In the series, the children
were never mentioned again.

The theme music heard on *Curb Your Enthusiasm* is called *Frolic* and was written by Italian composer Luciano Michelini. Larry David discovered it while watching a bank advertisement, years before he created the show.

In 2003, Juan Catalan was cleared of premeditated murder charges against a material witness (a felony eligible for capital punishment) only after cut-out footage shot for the "Carpool Lane" episode of *Curb Your Enthusiasm* showed him (and his daughter) attending a Los Angeles Dodgers baseball game some 20 miles from the scene of the crime.

Struggling to come up with plotlines for the third season of *Felicity*, creator J.J. Abrams, who was aware of the CIA program that recruits college kids to be spies, half-jokingly suggested to his writers that they consider having the title character spend her summer as a government agent, then return to school the next fall as if nothing had ever happened. Everyone laughed at the notion, but Abrams had the last laugh when he turned the idea into the series *Alias*.

In 1998, Max Mutchnick and David Kohan pitched NBC a standard couples comedy in which a gay man and his straight female best friend were supporting characters. The network found the pair of pals—Will and Grace—more interesting than the leads, and suggested that they build the show around them.

The part of Monk was
originally written
for Michael Richards.

In *Smallville,*

Clark Kent always wears clothes

that are blue and red,

or at least one of those colors.

60 Minutes

is the only TV show with no

theme song or music.

The Magna Doodle that hung on the inside of the door to Joey and Chandler's apartment on *Friends* had a different picture on it every episode. There was usually some tenuous connection between the drawing and the plot of the episode.

The single longest-running commercial in television history is the ad for Life cereal featuring Mikey ("Let Mikey try it. He hates everything."), which aired nationally for 12 years.

Struggling to create a new ad campaign for Kellogg's Raisin Bran, ad exec Danny Nichols took a box of the product home, then spent the evening analyzing it, trying to single out those qualities that separated this brand from the pack. As a matter of course, he dumped the contents onto his kitchen table and began to play with them. Grabbing a miniature scoop he used to measure out coffee, he filled it with raisins. Twice. The next day, when asked by his agency if he had come up with anything, he informed them that he had. "There are two scoops of raisins in every box," he announced.

Tony the Tiger made his debut in 1952 as part of a plan for a series of animal illustrations appearing on boxes of Sugar Frosted Flakes. Other animals were to include Katie the Kangaroo, Elmo the Elephant, and Newt the Gnu. Supposedly, Kellogg's goal was to have a character for every letter of the alphabet but thanks to a *Gr-r-reat!* slogan, Tony grabbed the spotlight, and the rest quickly faded into advertising history.

Soon after launching
Franken Berry in 1971, General Mills
was forced to recall the product and
pull it from supermarket shelves.
Seems that after eating it,
when kids went to the bathroom,
their poop had turned pink from
the food coloring.

Grape Nuts are neither grape nor nuts; rather, they are made from wheat and barley. The inventor, C. W. Post, came up with the name because the cereal contained maltose (which he incorrectly thought was grape sugar) and because the distinctive flavor reminded him of nuts.

Henry Perky, a lawyer with stomach problems, built a contraption that would press boiled wheat into filaments, which could then be shaped and baked into easily digestible biscuits. Hoping to sell his patented "cereal machine" to others who also suffered from dyspepsia, he rode around in a horse-drawn carriage, passing out free samples of the dried wheat snack his invention could make. However, when it quickly became clear that it was the pillow-shaped biscuits—and not the appliance—that people wanted to buy, Perky dropped plans to market the machine, and opened a bakery called the Shredded Wheat Company.

The technical (copyrighted) name for the mini marshmallows found in Lucky Charms (and other breakfast cereals) is Marbits. They were invented, as was the cereal, by General Mills VP John Holahan, when he cut up a few orange marshmallow Circus Peanuts, stirred them into a bowl of Cheerios, and was impressed with the results.

A clinician in Minneapolis was mixing a batch of bran gruel for his patients when some of the mix accidentally spilled on the hot stove, crackling and sizzling into a crisp flake. He tasted the result and, realizing the accident had promise, took his discovery to the Washburn Crosby Company—which, in 1921, developed it for market and called the product Wheaties.

The first athlete to appear on a Wheaties box was baseball great Lou Gehrig in 1924.

Michael Jordan has been on
the Wheaties box more
than any other athlete—18 times,
including three appearances
with the NBA champion
Chicago Bulls.

In 1937, Wheaties, which sponsored local baseball radio broadcasts on 95 stations around the country, held a nationwide contest to find its "most popular announcer." The winner was a play-by-play guy from WHO in Des Moines, Iowa, named Ronald Reagan. His prize was an all-expense-paid trip to California to visit the Chicago Cubs training camp; while there, he was spotted and asked to screen test for Warner Brothers.

A one-ounce
serving of Cheerios contains
400 individual "O's".

In 1997, among the workers earning $12 per hour sweeping up Cheerios dust from the floor of the General Mills factory in Cedar Rapids, Iowa, was a biochemical engineering student named Ashton Kutcher.

51

If the minimum wage
had kept pace with the rise in
executive salaries since 1990,
America's poorest-paid workers
would be making more than
$23 an hour.

The idea behind FedEx
originated in the 1965 term paper
Fred Smith wrote for an
undergraduate economics class
at Yale University.
He got a "C" for his efforts.

Ben Cohen and Jerry Greenfield wanted to go into the bagel business, but when they discovered that the equipment alone would cost $40,000, the two opted to take a $5 correspondence course in ice-cream making instead.

American Airlines
saved $40,000 in 1987 by
eliminating one olive
from each salad served
in first-class.

The first Sony product
was a rice cooker—
which tended to short out,
catch fire and emit
electrical shocks.

Sony's tiny cassette player-with-headphones invention didn't do that well when first released as the Soundabout in the U.S., and as the Stowaway in England. But sales took off after both countries adopted the same nonsensical name that the Japanese had successfully used for it: Walkman.

The star in the Macy's
logo was taken from a tattoo on
founder R.H. Macy's hand.

The flagship Bloomingdale's store (at 1000 Third Avenue, in Manhattan) is the third most popular tourist attraction in New York City, after the Empire State Building and the Statue of Liberty.

The Statue of Liberty's mouth is three feet wide.

X-rays of the *Mona Lisa*
show that there are three
completely different versions of the
same subject, also painted
by Leonardo Da Vinci, under
the final portrait.

Vincent van Gogh
sold only one painting in
his whole life—
and that was to his brother.

The "Thinker"
depicted in the famous statue
by Auguste Rodin is the
poet Dante.

Abby Rockefeller liked the window displays at Saks Fifth Avenue so much that she picked the designer, Donald Deskey, to do the interior spaces of Radio City Music Hall.

In 1961, Matisse's *Le Bateau* (The Boat) hung upside-down for two months at the Museum of Modern Art in New York City. None of the 116,000 visitors noticed.

Marvin Gardens is the only property on the Monopoly game board that is not named after a street. In actuality it is an upscale area in Atlantic County, New Jersey, which, had it been spelled correctly, should have been Marven Gardens.

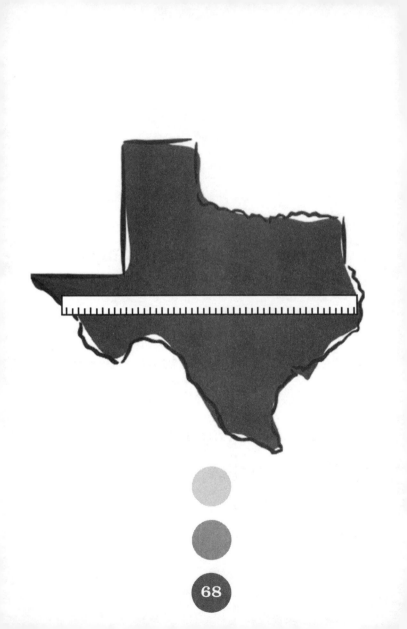

68

At the state's widest point,
the distance across Texas is greater
than the distance between
New York City and Chicago.

A dice game played by a wealthy Canadian couple aboard their boat proved so popular that they asked Edwin Lowe (of Bingo fame) if he would make up some samples for them to give as gifts. Lowe was so impressed with their "Yacht Game" that he offered to buy the rights. They agreed, sacrificing all future royalties for a few free copies of the game—a game Lowe manufactured and sold with great success under the catchier name Yahtzee.

Kites are named
after the kite bird, a member
of the hawk family.

Only female ants
(but never the queen; agricultural
regulations prohibit it) are what
Uncle Milton Industries mails out to
be used in its Ant Farm,
because male ants do not do well
in captivity.

A pair of married art students happened to notice that the vinyl they were using for a school project would automatically stick to the semigloss paint in their bathroom, so they cut out basic shapes and combined them to decorate the wall. They and their friends had so much fun adding to and rearranging this giant collage that they decided to scale down the idea and market it, calling their brainchild Colorforms.

All Crayola crayon names
appear on labels in lowercase
because tests reveal that lowercase
letters are easiest for elementary
school students to read.

The distinctive smell
that you experience upon opening a
box of crayons comes from
stearic acid—
which is the formal name for
processed beef fat.

The light bulb used to power the Easy-Bake Oven generates heat equal to 350 degrees. Which means that any recipe (as long as it fits into the small round pan and doesn't rise so much that it can't slide through the cooking chamber) that can be made in a regular oven at 350 degrees—can also be made in an Easy-Bake.

Hot Wheels are 1/64th scale
to their real-life counterparts and,
when going downhill, can reach
speeds of 300 mph.

Of the 20 possible answers on a Magic 8-Ball, ten are positive, five negative and five neutral. Which, according to statisticians, gives a high degree of accuracy to the ball's ability to forecast.

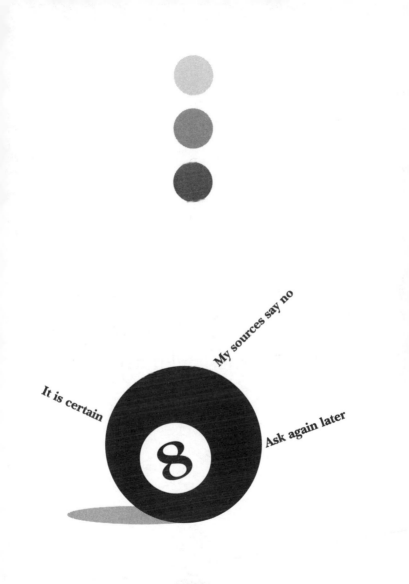

81

James and Arthur Ingoldsby, the brothers who formulated and created Magic Rocks, were pioneers in the health food business, and the men responsible for Tiger's Milk protein powder and nutrition bars.

A.C. Gilbert, the man
who invented the Erector Set, was
also a physician (Yale Medical
School) and a Gold Medalist
(in pole vaulting) at the 1908
Olympic Games.

Beyond lifting images off the pages of the Sunday funnies, Silly Putty has been used by pilots (as earplugs), secretaries (to clean typewriter keys), athletes (who squeeze it to strengthen their grip), dry cleaners (as a method to remove lint from clothing), restaurants (beats a matchbook for leveling the legs of a wobbly table), astronauts (to keep tools fastened down during weightlessness), and zookeepers (as a means of casting gorilla footprints needed for identification records).

In the late 1980s, there was a worldwide whoopee cushion shortage. Rubber manufacturers in the Far East who made the classic gag had to devote their entire workforce to the production of surgical gloves and condoms in order to meet the increased demand created by the AIDS crisis. As a result, for approximately two years, there was no time left for making whoopees.

Tinkertoy was invented by a tombstone designer and salesman who decided to try his hand at toy making when he noticed how much fun his own children had sticking pencils into empty spools of thread, then haphazardly assembling them into all sorts of abstract forms.

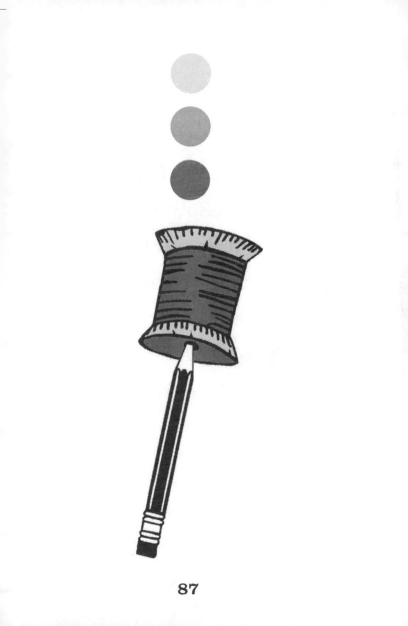

Tonka Toys was founded in Mound, Minnesota—and took its name from nearby Lake Minnetonka. The word "tonka" also means "great" in Dakota Sioux, the language of the American Indian tribe native to the area.

While every View-Master
reel has 14 frames, each contains
only seven different images, since
seeing in 3-D requires one
visual for each eye.
Packets normally contain
three reels, so a story has to
be told in 21 scenes.

There are 2,598,960 possible hands in a five-card poker game.

In a random group
of 23 people,
odds are that
two will share the
same birthday.

If a penny is randomly tossed into the air, the odds are actually one percent higher that it will land on tails as opposed to heads. This is because the image of Lincoln on the heads side weighs more, which slightly increases the chances that it will end up on the bottom.

The cost to mint a
penny is more than one cent.

In the U.S.,
more gold is used to make
class rings than any
other piece of jewelry.

The House of Fabergé made
only 50 of its jewel-encrusted eggs.
Of the 50, 28 are in museums,
14 are in private hands (including
the nine that had been owned
by the late Malcolm Forbes),
and eight are missing.

The highest price ever paid for an item listed on eBay was $4.9 million— for a Gulfstream II Jet.

The 'k' in $10k (or any other
monetary figure measured in
thousand-dollar increments) comes
from the scientific abbreviation for
kilo, which is a derivative
of the Greek word *khiloi,* meaning
"one thousand."

Not counting vowels,
the most frequently used letter in
the English language is *t*.

The # symbol on
the pound key is called
an *octothorpe*.

The saying "in like Flynn" refers to actor Errol Flynn and his acquittal on statutory rape charges.

In chess, the term "checkmate" comes from the Persian phrase *Shah Mat*, which means "the king is dead".

The expression "knuckle down"
originated with marbles;
players put knuckles to the ground
for their best shots.

The popular urban sportswear clothier FUBU is an acronym for *For Us By Us*.

The notion that someone is "mad as a hatter," as well as Alice in Wonderland's Mad Hatter, stems from the fact that in the early 19th century, felt hat makers used mercury to stabilize wool. As a result, many of them became poisoned by the fumes, developing uncontrollable tremors, confused speech and hallucinations.

Beef Jerky got its
name from *charki*, the Inca word
for "dried llama meat".

The avocado is indigenous to Central America and, because of its shape, derives its name from the Aztec word *ahuacatl*—meaning "testicle".

The grapefruit

was not named for how it tastes,

but for the way it grows—

in bunches.

Unlike most fresh fruits,

grapes will

not float in Jell-O.

Cochineal and carminic acid, popular colorants used to impart a deep red shade to fruit juices, gelatins, ice creams and candies, are made from ground beetles.

In 1905, eleven-year-old Frank Epperson mixed up some popular fruit-flavored soda powder and inadvertently left the glass outside overnight. When he awoke the next morning, he found the stirring stick frozen upright in his drink, and proudly showed his friends this unique "soda on a stick." Eighteen years later, Epperson patented the Popsicle.

There are 216 noodles
in a can of Campbell's Chicken
Noodle Soup.

By the time a kid graduates from high school, he will have eaten 1,500 peanut butter sandwiches.

The color of the plastic tab used to close a loaf of bread indicates the day it was delivered fresh to the store. While the colors can vary regionally, traditionally they run alphabetically, which means blue was delivered on Monday, green on Tuesday, orange on Wednesday, red on Thursday, white on Friday and yellow on Saturday.

Asked to make a special dish to mark the Naples visit of Queen Margherita Teresa Giovanni of Italy in 1889, tavern owner Don Raffaele Esposito took a traditional oven-baked flatbread (known as pizza) and, instead of brushing it with the expected basics (olive oil, herbs, and spices), he layered it with fresh tomatoes, a cheese made from the milk of water buffalo, and basil—because those ingredients were red, white and green, the colors of the Italian flag. The queen loved it, and Margherita pizza was soon a menu staple all over Southern Italy.

According to the staffs at the Domino's Pizza locations in (and around) Washington, D.C., if there is a marked increase in the number of late night deliveries to the White House or the Pentagon, it usually signifies that a major news announcement of national importance will follow in 48 to 72 hours.

The record for the most pizzas delivered nationwide in one evening was set on June 17, 1994, as O.J. Simpson fled in his Ford Bronco down the Los Angeles freeways and Americans couldn't take their eyes off their television sets.

NECCO stands for the

New **E**ngland **C**onfectionery **CO**mpany

—which is the corporation

that manufactures and distributes

the candy.

Cashews are not sold in their shells because the oil that surrounds the shell is highly irritating to the skin, and peeling the nuts by hand can cause blisters.

Saffron is the dried
threadlike stigma of the violet-colored
crocus plant. Its high cost is due to the
fact that the crocus only blooms for
two weeks each autumn,
each bloom has only three stigmas,
and it takes about 225,000 stigmas to
yield one pound.

Onions get their distinctive smell by soaking up sulfur from the soil. These sulfoxides, which form a mild sulfuric acid when they combine with the water in our eyes, are also what cause most of us to cry while chopping onions.

Immigrants arriving at
Ellis Island were served ice cream
as part of their first American meal.
Baffled, many attempted
to spread it on their bread.

After inventing and patenting a small appliance that automatically mixed drinks, F.J. Osius had no means, nor the money, to promote and finance its sale. So he went to Fred Waring, a popular bandleader who had a fascination with new gadgets, and convinced him to market the creation to the numerous hotels and restaurants he would visit on tour. Waring agreed, and Osius' drink mixer became known as the Waring Blender.

Champagne actually gets people tipsy faster than other alcoholic beverages because the carbon dioxide bubbles speed the alcohol into the bloodstream.

You can use a
drop of vodka on each lens
to clean eyeglasses
without streaks.

One 12-ounce glass
of soda contains
up to ten teaspoons
of sugar.

Robert Cade, a University of Florida physiology professor, was determined to create a liquid that could quickly replace body fluids lost due to physical exertion and hot weather, so he developed a sports drink and tested it on ten of his school's football players. The team—the Gators—posted a winning record that season, and, as a result, people took to calling Cade's concoction Gatorade.

132

The football huddle
was conceived by a deaf quarterback
at Gallaudet University who used
sign language to communicate.
Not wanting the opposition to see
his signals, the team would bunch
together to shield him.

When the University of Nebraska Cornhuskers play football at home, their stadium (which holds a crowd of 16,000 people) becomes the state's third largest city.

The Kentucky Derby is
the oldest continually held sports
event in the United States; the
second oldest is the Westminster
Kennel Club dog show.

The Olympic gold medal

is actually an Olympic silver medal

gilded with six grams

(approximately one-quarter ounce)

of pure gold.

The silhouette on
the NBA logo is a portrait of
Jerry West.

Initially, the numbers
put on baseball uniforms were
done in accordance with
the player's position in his team's
batting order, so Babe Ruth
became 3, Lou Gehrig was 4, etc.

The nine-foot statue of Babe
Ruth at Baltimore's Oriole Park
shows him leaning on his
bat and clutching a right-handed
glove. Which is strange, given that
the baseball great was a lefty.

A bowling pin

need only tilt 7.5 degrees in

order to fall down.

Richard Nixon was
an avid—and accomplished—
bowler.

The picture of the meeting between
Richard Nixon and Elvis Presley
in 1970 is among the most requested
photographs (from the millions)
in the holdings of the National
Archives and Records Administration
in Washington, D.C., ranking up
there with images of Pearl Harbor,
D-day, and Hiroshima.

The autopsy of John Dillinger revealed his physical endowment to be normal. It was a morgue photograph of his body—in which his arm was positioned under the sheet, creating a noticeable bulge—that led to the legend that his male organ was so unusually large it had been kept by the Smithsonian for its collections.

Dr. William Moulton Marston,
the Harvard psychologist
who invented the lie detector, also
created *Wonder Woman*.

Ronald McDonald is
considered the second most
recognizable character in the world,
after Santa Claus, and ahead of
Mickey Mouse.

Walt Disney was
afraid of mice.

147

People who work at Disneyland are not referred to as employees; rather, they are called "cast members". Cast members who don a character costume and walk around the park greeting guests refer to that as having "duck duty". They also refer to It's A Small World as "the asylum," on the theory that that's where they'll end up as a result of repeated (over)exposure to the song.

After an endless meeting, and still unable to come up with a name for the monorail being built for the San Diego Zoo's Wild Animal Park, chief designer Chuck Faust threw up his hands and, as a joke, scribbled down WGASA on the plans. Because it sounded African, it stuck (and the system is known to this day as the WGASA Bush Line)—but in truth, the **W**orld's **G**reatest **A**nimal **S**how **A**nywhere got its name from the acronym for *Who gives a s**t anyway?*

The sound of fingernails on a blackboard is similar in frequency to the danger cries of some jungle primates. It is this similarity—hardwired into our biological makeup long ago—that scientists believe causes nearly every human to have such a strong (negative) reaction to it.

Rats have sex up to
20 times a day.

A cockroach has

two brains.

Only male canaries

can sing.

Barry Manilow had a big hit with *I Write the Songs*, but despite the title, and a very prolific songwriting career, he actually didn't write it. Beach Boy Bruce Johnston did, in honor of his pal Brian Wilson—who really DID write the songs that made the whole world sing, including *California Girls*, *Surf City*, *I Get Around*, *Wouldn't It Be Nice*, and *Good Vibrations*.

The term *piano* is
short for the instrument's full name,
piano et forte—which translates to
"soft and loud".

Hip hop artists Kid 'N Play, female rappers Salt-N-Pepa, and comic Martin Lawrence all worked together in the early 1980s—at a Sears store in Queens, New York.

Roger McGuinn, leader of the Byrds, started the 1960s granny glasses craze when he found a pair at a secondhand clothing store and bought them so he'd have something to shield his eyes from the glare of the lights during a performance.

KISS co-founder Gene Simmons
not only discovered Van Halen,
he also managed Liza Minnelli's
recording career.

Unlike vinyl records,
a CD begins playing near the
center and spirals outward
toward the edge.

163

It isn't that manufacturers can't record on both sides of a CD or a DVD—it's that they don't. The general industry preference is to give consumers a colorful label on one side, as opposed to a two-sided disc with twice the capacity.

The cost to manufacture
an Oscar is $300, compared with
$900 for an Emmy—
and only $100 for the
Pulitzer Prize.

Success doesn't come cheap.
If selected to receive a star on the
Hollywood Walk of Fame, the
honored celebrity must pony up
$15,000 for the privilege. The fee is
usually paid by a sponsor—such as
a movie studio, television network,
or record company—that stands
to benefit from the resulting
media attention.

Empty boxes of movie candies
can no longer be turned into
makeshift kazoos because of the
glue used to seal the end flaps—
a result of stricter safety
measures following the Tylenol
scare in the early 1980s.

The bulk of the money made
by movie theatres
comes from selling snacks,
not showing films.

There is a
Starbucks coffee cup
visible in every scene
in *Fight Club*.

Legally Blonde runs
only 96 minutes, yet
Reese Witherspoon wears
40 different hairstyles.

Early drafts of the original *Toy Story* featured a Barbie character, but the role eventually went to Little Bo Peep when Mattel refused to allow its doll's likeness to be used in the film. However, given the huge popularity of the movie, plus the substantial boost in sales of those toys that were featured in it, Mattel was quick to sign off for the sequel, and (Tour Guide) Barbie was included in *Toy Story 2*.

In the scene in *Toy Story 2* where Tour Guide Barbie cuts loose and dances, animators modeled her moves after Ann-Margret's moves in *Viva Las Vegas*.

In *Monsters, Inc.*, Sulley's fur contained more than 2,320,413 individually animated hairs. On average, it took 11 hours for the artists to render a single frame of the character.

Shrek is Yiddish

for monster.

Director/star George Clooney opted to use archive footage of Joseph McCarthy in *Good Night, and Good Luck*, instead of casting an actor to portray the senator and re-create the hearings. When the movie underwent test screenings, audience members left comment cards stating that whoever had played McCarthy "overacted" and "wasn't believable," not realizing that it was the real McCarthy they had been watching.

On the first day of production of his first film, *sex, lies, and videotape*, Steven Soderbergh received a telegram from the producers. In it, they taunted him good-naturedly, telling him that they were ignoring the reports they had heard, that he couldn't even direct traffic. Twelve years later, Soderbergh won an Oscar…for directing *Traffic*.

Director Robert Altman did not want kids—especially teenage boys—to see his film *Gosford Park*, knowing that they wouldn't like it and that their presence in the theatre would disturb those who did. So he purposely included the F-word a handful of times, to ensure an R rating and to assure himself that no teenagers would be allowed in.

In the original story that inspired *Eyes Wide Shut*, the family name of Tom Cruise's character, Bill, who was Jewish, was Scheuer. However, when director Stanley Kubrick insisted that Bill and wife Alice be "vanilla Americans" and a bit like Harrison Ford, screenwriter Frederic Raphael changed Cruise's character's name from Scheuer...to Harford.

The *Rhapsody in Blue* segment from *Fantasia 2000* was done in the style of caricaturist Al Hirschfeld, who was famous for incorporating the name of his daughter Nina into his drawings. In homage to the artist, "Nina" can be found three times in the animation as well: on the end of Duke's toothpaste tube, in the fur collar of John's wife, and in her hair.

The international corporation set up by Saddam Hussein to launder money from his various enterprises was called Montana Management—after Tony Montana, the character Al Pacino played in *Scarface*.

The "tornado" in
The Wizard of Oz was a 35-foot-long
muslin stocking,
photographed over miniatures of a
Kansas farm and fields.

The Wizard of Oz's
complete name was Oscar Zoroaster
Phadrig Isaac Norman Henkle
Emmanuel Ambroise Diggs;
the initials (purposely) spell out
O.Z.P.I.N.H.E.A.D.

J.R.R. Tolkien wrote
The Lord of the Rings as a single
volume, and was annoyed
when it was published in the
mid-1950s as a trilogy.

In 1968, J.R.R. Tolkien sold
the film rights to
The Lord of the Rings
for $15,000.

The New Zealand government appointed a Minister for Lord of the Rings, whose sole job was to exploit as many monetary opportunities from the films that he could.

In early 2003, writer/producer Joel Surnow read an advance copy of *The Da Vinci Code* and thought it would provide a great storyline for the third season of his hit show, *24*. Surnow asked his boss, Brian Grazer, about acquiring the film rights to the book. Author Dan Brown had no intention of his book being adapted for a TV show, and rejected their bid. A few months later, Sony Pictures paid $6 million for the book—and hired Grazer to produce it.

Sir Arthur Conan Doyle studied to be a doctor at the University of Edinburgh in Scotland, where he was greatly influenced by a professor who used deductive reasoning to diagnose disease. Upon graduation, Doyle opened an office in Hampshire; when the practice failed to generate enough patients, he would pass the time by writing detective stories.

190

Sherlock Holmes was
named after American poet
Oliver Wendell Holmes and cricket
player Mordecai Sherlock.

Ian Fleming was
an ardent bird-watcher and
named his most famous
character after noted bird field
guide author, James Bond.

192

Kay Thompson based
her popular *Eloise* children's
books on her own godchild—
Liza Minnelli.

In an attempt to save money on the company's annual holiday promotion, executives at Montgomery Ward stores asked Robert May, one of their copywriters, to come up with a children's story that they could print themselves, instead of having to buy existing coloring books to give away. The plan paid off: that Christmas they distributed 2.4 million copies of May's tale, which featured an underdog (named Rudolph) who had been ostracized by his reindeer community because of his glowing red nose.

Dr. Seuss' first book, *And to Think That I Saw It on Mulberry Street,* was rejected 27 times before he stepped into an office elevator and bumped into an old friend who happened to be working at a publishing house.

Dr. Seuss wrote
Green Eggs and Ham after being
challenged by Bennett Cerf
(his editor) to produce a
book using fewer than fifty
different words.

Robert Louis Stevenson, suffering from advanced tuberculosis, wrote his 60,000-word novel, *Dr. Jekyll and Mr. Hyde* in six days.

Barbara Cartland had 723 novels published in her lifetime (more than any other author)—and left behind 160 completed manuscripts.

The most William Shakespeare earned for writing a play was eight pounds ($1, 325 by today's economic standard), never making more than an annual income of 20 pounds ($3,313) from his writing. Luckily, he inherited real estate and his acting career paid well.

200

According to a recent survey,
only 56.6 percent of Americans say
that they read a book of any
kind last year.

Researchers can now add one more
person to the list.

David Hoffman is a television writer, a frequent on-camera correspondent, and the author of seven books about popular culture—for which, in recent years, he has been paid to play with toys, challenge untapped cooking skills (with the help of some big-name chefs), and eat and shop his way across the country.

He lives in Los Angeles, where he likes to pretend this is hard work.